*f*P

## Also by Gary Zukav

*The Dancing Wu Li Masters:*
*An Overview of the New Physics*

*The Seat of the Soul*

*Thoughts from the Seat of the Soul:*
*Meditations for Souls in Process*

*Soul Stories*

*Soul to Soul:*
*Communications from the Heart*

## With Linda Francis

*The Heart of the Soul:*
*Emotional Awareness*

*Thoughts from the Heart of the Soul:*
*Meditations on Emotional Awareness*

*The Mind of the Soul:*
*Responsible Choice*

*Self-Empowerment Journal:*
*A Companion to the Mind of the Soul*

# Soul to Soul

## Meditations

Daily Reflections
for Spiritual Growth

## GARY ZUKAV

FREE PRESS

NEW YORK   LONDON   TORONTO   SYDNEY

*f*P

FREE PRESS

A Division of Simon & Schuster, Inc.
1230 Avenue of the Americas
New York, NY 10020

First Free Press trade paper edition March 2008

FREE PRESS and colophon are trademarks of
Simon & Schuster, Inc.

For information about special discounts for bulk purchases,
please contact Simon & Schuster Special Sales at
1-800-456-6798 or business@simonandschuster.com.

Manufactured in the United States of America

10 9 8 7 6 5 4 3 2 1

Library of Congress Cataloging-in-Publication

Zukav, Gary.
Soul to soul meditations : daily reflections for spiritual growth /
Gary Zukav.
p. cm.
1. Meditations. 2. New Age movement. I. Title.
BP605.N48Z8537 2008
204'.32—dc22          2007046201

ISBN-13: 978-1-4166-6956-5
ISBN-10:     1-4166-6956-1

This book is dedicated with
love and appreciation to Linda Francis,
my spiritual partner, playmate,
and co-creator.

# PREFACE

Welcome to this collection of soul-to-soul meditations. The book is small in size, but no soul-to-soul communication is small. What is more important than the purpose of your existence, and how you can use it to contribute to Life?

Each thought in this book invites your consideration, invokes your wisdom, and feeds your compassion. All soul-to-soul communications do this. How many of your communications are soul to soul? How many do you want to be? As you read the thoughts in this book, pay attention to your own. Allow your own wisdom to begin to guide you, and as you do, more and more of your thoughts and communications will become soul to soul.

I also encourage you to read the book these thoughts come from, *Soul to Soul: Communications from the Heart,* and visit www.seatofthesoul.com. Both will support you in living your life soul to soul.

Love,
Gary Zukav

# Soul to Soul
## Meditations

Your heart is your home and all roads lead to home.

A Soul Subject is not a mental creation. It is a perception that resonates with a deeper part of yourself than the intellect can reach.

A Soul Subject is a multisensory perception. It is an observation of physical circumstances plus a recognition of what they mean.

We live in a world of meaning. That world is the Earth school, the physical arena of our personal and collective experiences. We are the students. Our experiences are the curriculum.

Our personal and collective experiences constitute our Soul Subjects.

See how the sun moves from north to south and back again, and from low in the sky to high, and then down again as the seasons change. Live a complete cycle with nature.

Watch the grass in the meadows turn from green to brown, and then disappear under the snow. Watch the streams freeze, thaw, and run freely again with butterflies playing over them. Enrich yourself with every detail.

When you strive for balance, be gentle with yourself. How can you recognize balance without recognizing imbalance?

If you strive only to avoid the darkness or to cling to the light, you cannot live in balance. Try striving to be conscious of all that you are.

It is not only things going wrong that frighten us. It is also our lives going profoundly right. It is clarity piercing the armor of encrusted prejudices—about others and ourselves.

The birth of new life is as challenging as it is exhilarating, as frightening as it is liberating. Are you prepared to leave old fears, angers, and judgments behind?

Spiritual growth is not an easy escape from the painful circumstances of your life. It begins with an eyes-open exploration of them and their cause. You are the cause. Every insight that brings you to this realization is a new beginning.

Letting go of your familiar props—your righteous judgments, unchallenged beliefs, and feelings of superiority or inferiority—places you in new territory. The old is gone and everything that is emerging is new.

You cannot grow spiritually and re-main the same. Understanding that is knowledge. Seeing it is wisdom.

One special day in June the sun is higher in the sky than it is at any other time of the year. That day is also the longest day of the year. It is the summer solstice. Maximal potential has become maximal growth, as it has before and as it will again.

Honor the insights that appear to you.

As the seasons of your life come and go, acknowledge the shifts that happen in you and allow them to mature in their own time.

The fullness of your most noble and healthy aspirations will come, just as the fall harvest always comes.

First come the sprouts, then growth and maturation, and then the harvest. Let wisdom and love sprout and grow in you the same way.

In the northern hemisphere the deepest moment of the winter comes not in January or February but in December, when the night is longest and the day is shortest. It is the winter solstice. The winter solstice is a very powerful time in the cycle of life and death, death and rebirth, disintegration and renewal that controls all Life on the Earth.

The contraction of energy that the long nights and cold days reflect reaches its limit at the winter solstice and a cycle completes itself. From that moment forward, even though the winter remains to unfold as it must, the spring has been born, and the summer and the harvests of the summer that follow.

The dark and trying season of winter is repeated in your life again and again. Each tragedy, loss, failure, and humiliation reaches its inmost movement, spends its energy, and from that long journey another begins—a journey toward warmth, light, and expansion.

The arrival of winter, the coming of darkness and death, initiates the coming of light and life. This cycle controls the unfolding of your life and all within it.

You cannot stop the death that comes in the winter nor the life that comes with the summer, but you can determine in the winter what will be born in the summer.

This is the power of deep winter—it challenges you, confronts you, and shows you what you must change in yourself.

Deep winter is your potential beckoning to you, disguised as an adversary, a tragedy, or a disaster.

Will your fears overwhelm you, or will they show you new and different ways to respond to them?

Life is like a buffalo's breath on a cold winter day. It is there, and then it's gone.

L ife comes and goes like the cloud of a moist breath on a frosty morning.

The journey that all of us are on is the journey from Love to Love. What happens between the beginning and the end of the journey is your life.

Joy, sorrow, care, courage, and tenderness are real. Kindness is real. Tears are real, and so is laughter. These are the currency of the heart. They are meant to be exchanged.

Love goes beyond warm feelings and connected moments. It is looking for what is needed and providing it. It is living directly from the heart without reservation.

L ove is leaving behind expectations of acknowledgment, praise, and appreciation. It is honoring your inner sense of appropriateness and committing the full force of your being to it.

Y‌ou are bonded to your fellow students in the Earth school by your
love for Life.

Look for something fundamental to value in others. Not a characteristic, such as "You are so charming," but something meaningful, such as "I appreciate how you take strong stands without making people wrong," and "I feel safe around you because I know you are listening."

What can you say to someone that is so meaningful he will carry it with him unto death? Only a message from the heart can reach that deep, heal that powerfully, and last that long.

Openness to others as you would like others to be open to you is love.

L ove is feeling the pain of others as if it were your own, and acting accordingly.

Restricting your love to your family, or to those you know, or those who look, think, act, dress, and speak like you, prevents you from experiencing your ability to love.

L ove is a fire that is out of control.

Once love is ignited, it cannot be contained. You may strive for moderation in diet, exercise, and work, but striving for moderation in love is like striving for moderation in breathing.

Practice moderation in all things except love.

Fear becomes comfortable, even though it is painful, if it stays long enough. So does jealousy, greed, and vengefulness. They begin to appear as old friends, like old clothing that feels natural because you have worn it a long time.

Your painful emotions are designed to bring your attention to the parts of your personality that you were born to challenge and change, so that you can transform yourself from an angry, jealous, avaricious, or vengeful person into one who is compassionate, wise, and grateful for Life.

You can shed your anger, jealousy, hatred of yourself or others, greed, and every other painful emotion just like a snake sheds its skin.

We are all on the journey from emotional avoidance to emotional awareness, from victimhood to responsibility, and from anger to compassion. We do not have the choice to take the journey or not. We have only the choices of when we will begin the journey and how we will treat ourselves and one another along the way.

The painful feeling of unworthiness lies at the heart of human experience. It is the pain of not being good enough, attractive enough, or human enough. It is the fear of being seen for who you really are, and rejected.

What emotional reaction controls your thoughts and perceptions when you feel powerless—unloved and unlovable? Is it disdain and superiority, emotional withdrawal, jealousy, rage, or fear?

Instead of assuming what makes you feel worst, assume what makes you feel best. You are free to make the most positive assumption as well as the most negative.

Creating authentic power—the alignment of your personality with your soul—requires discovering the parts of your personality that are creating destructive consequences and changing them.

The magnetic field of fear calls to you every day. It is the need to be right or righteous, to make other people wrong, to criticize, overeat, buy what you don't need, misuse drugs, or have another drink. It is every obsessive, compulsive, and addictive impulse.

Whenever you focus your thoughts on how precious Life is, your life will become so meaningful to you that you will savor it.

When the pain of continuing a destructive behavior exceeds the pain of stopping, a threshold is crossed. What seemed unthinkable becomes thinkable.

Each moment is a moment of choice—a time to leave the old, the limited, the restrained, and the contracted for the new, the unbound, and the liberating potential that expands before you.

If you hate those who hate, you become like them.

If you can look with compassion upon those who have suffered and those who have committed acts of cruelty alike, then you will see that all are suffering. The remedy for suffering is not to inflict more suffering.

A new life is calling you. It is the birth of a new species that longs to occur in each of us. It is an attraction to harmony, cooperation, sharing, and reverence for Life that did not exist before. It is sensing, seeing, feeling, or hearing intelligence, wisdom, and compassion that you were not aware of before.

Can you recognize when you are creating consequences you do not want, and choose differently, even while you feel the impulse to shout, withdraw emotionally, seek revenge, criticize, or any of the other ways that you have created painful consequences in the past? Doing that is creating authentic power, and no one can do it for you.

Beauty surrounds you continually. Sometimes you see it only when you are about to leave it.

Experiment with taking the time to appreciate the beauty of your life before you are about to leave it.

W here a life of less awareness once unfolded unconsciously, a new life may emerge. New goals appear, and new ways of relating lead you to them. New satisfactions, never before considered, fulfill in unexpected ways. Meaning pervades all that you do, and joy carries you forward like a leaf on a river.

Your life can explode with potential that had little possibility of developing the day before, if you are open to it.

I f you distract yourself with questions such as "Why me?" and "Why is the universe so unfair?" you will not be able to make the shift in perspective that will allow you to value every experience in your life, and not only those that you approve.

From the perspective of your soul, the experiences of your life are neither good nor bad. They are neither just nor unjust. They are what they need to be, given the wisdom of the choices that you have made.

Each experience is an opportunity for you to learn in the intimacy of your own experience what you have created in the past, and choose to create differently.

As you develop new awareness, your values change. When that happens, you become uncomfortable expressing yourself in old ways and pursuing old goals.

Waking up to your humanity in a world that considers life a cheap commodity creates challenges that did not exist before.

Resenting the injustices in your life, raging against the unfairness of your experiences, and longing for circumstances to be other than they are, are fruitless tasks.

The journey you are on is deep and powerful. Your roots go far below the surface of appearances. Your infancy, childhood, adulthood, and old age are phases in the development of a plant. The plant will wither and die, but the root will remain.

I f you do not remember your soul, your death will appear catastrophic and final.

When you think photos in news-papers reveal who individuals are, you cannot appreciate the depth and power of the journey they are on, or the depth and power of the journey you are on.

When you look into a mirror, ask yourself, "Who is on this journey?"

re you more flexible than last year, or more rigid? Do you think more about your own needs than you did last year, or more about the needs of others?

Some individuals see the world as merciless and uncaring while others see it as wise and compassionate, and they have different experiences as a result.

very expectation is a reach too far. Every fall is a lesson. Learn the art of letting whatever is beyond your reach remain there, no matter how appealing or important it appears. When that happens, you will stand in your center.

No wind can bring the fruit down before it is ready to fall, and when it is ready to fall, nothing can keep it on the branch. The process has its own timing, and it creates changes in your life when those changes need to happen.

Picking blackberries without getting caught on the thorns, and knowing how to release yourself when you do, is part of a learning experience that has more value than putting berries on the table.

How many times have you gotten caught in a circumstance, tried to pull away without taking time to assess your situation, and been injured? Sometimes your circumstances will not release you until you stop, relax, and move with the flow. If you react to your circumstances without thinking, you make things worse.

U nlocking your heart is not something that happens once and is done
with. It is a moment-to-moment process
that will not stop until you die.

What would you do differently if you could feel the pain of others and the joy of others? What does your heart say to you at the thought that you can? What does it say to you at the thought that eventually you will?

How would you begin the process of living with awareness in a world in which the hurt of one is the hurt of all, and the honor of one is the honor of all?

We were born to touch each other. What does your touch feel like to others? Do you reach out in anger, disdain, or resentment? Do you need to please, or need to push away? Can you do what is appropriate, act with an open heart, and trust the Universe?

What are you sharing, and who is it enriching?

You cannot change the perception in someone else of a brother or sister as inhuman. The work that is necessary to change that picture requires your courage and your heart. It requires you to see clearly the brutality that pervades the human experience, and to change it in the only place you can change it permanently—in yourself.

The things that you don't like about yourself are the same things that you don't like about other people. The way that you treat yourself is also the way that you treat other people.

If you think you are unlovable, you won't be able to imagine that anyone else could think he is lovable either. If you love yourself, you will love other people.

How you feel about yourself is more than a private internal matter. It determines how you are with others and, ultimately, how you are with the Universe.

No one, not even nonphysical Teachers, know the decisions you will make as you encounter the circumstances of your life.

Souls agree to provide one another opportunities, in certain circumstances that might occur in the Earth school, to learn the lessons that each incarnates to learn and to give the gifts that each was born to give. They do not know how their personalities will choose to respond, but they agree to provide the opportunities to make choices.

For spiritual growth you must first build a foundation. You may want to spring into a new life of kindness and compassion, a life that is grounded and appropriate in every way, but until you build the foundation to support such a life, you will not be able to accomplish it.

Commitment to your spiritual growth
is the heart of spiritual growth.

Your emotional health and your spiritual development cannot be separated. You cannot be angry, resentful, jealous, and live in violent fantasies and negative judgments and be compassionate and kind at the same time.

Sensations are different from the labels of sensations. Labels are thoughts that occur in your mind. Sensations happen in your body.

As you journey through your life, do you see difficulties as obstacles, or as experiences that show you where to go, and how to change your course so that you will reach your goal?

When you resist your painful experiences, you ignore the guidance
they offer.

Your destination is a life of meaning, fulfillment, creativity, and joy—a life free of your fears, obsessions, compulsions, and addictions, without the insecurities that others activate so easily and the torments they create in you.

An intention is your reason, or motivation, for acting. It is the consciousness behind your action.

Even when you think you know your intention, you may have other intentions that you are not aware of and, if so, they will shape your experiences. Unconscious intentions are hidden agendas.

Searching for your hidden agendas is worth the effort. Before you speak, or act, ask yourself, "What is my intention?" and listen for an answer. Then you can decide to keep your intention or change it. In other words, you can consciously choose the experience you will create.

Can you find in yourself the same violence that you fear or disdain in other people? If you can, you will not judge others so harshly, even those who are violent, and you will begin the process of creating a world without violence, or at least with less violence.

The bonds that connect us exist moment to moment, whether we are aware of them or not. When we become aware of them, resentment turns to gratitude, anger becomes compassion, and the perception of senselessness becomes the experience of meaning.

Awareness of the bonds that connect us is multisensory perception. Appreciating them is reverence. Striving to behave accordingly is the pursuit of authentic power.

Every life in the Earth school is perfect, including your own, even if it is not the way you think it ought to be.

What choices are you making about your life? Are you listening to what your life is telling you, or to what others are telling you about your life?

What in your life is tormenting you? What circumstances are you resisting? What situations are you regretting? Do you say things like, "If only this had not happened?" "If only I had not . . ."

Examine your life closely. It may take you a long time to see the grace in your difficult experiences, and to use that grace to transform and enrich your life, but it is worth the effort.

You must distinguish between what is urgent and what is important. You could accomplish all of the urgent things that you desire without accomplishing anything that is important.

Ponder the depth and the power of loyalty—the ability to serve and support a cause greater than yourself.

When humanity was limited in its perceptions to the five senses, the greatest cause for most individuals was family, tribe, community, or nation. For others it was a belief, or an idea. Now that we are expanding beyond the limitations of the five senses, the greater cause for all is becoming Life—Life that includes all living things, all things that do not appear to be living, all thoughts, all actions, all customs, all beliefs, and all colors.

Loyalty to Life brings together cultures, nations, tribes, races, and religions. It is the only idea that springs from the heart, not from the mind.

Millions of humans are becoming aware of themselves as threads in a larger fabric of Life, and moving with deep dedication to contribute all that they are to it.

When great herds of buffalo migrated across the high plains, the calves were always at the center of the herd, where they were protected. The old buffalos moved to the outside of the herd and offered themselves to their brothers, the wolves, in order to keep the young safe. We can learn from them to become better humans. Perhaps we are all old buffalos in training.

Do you have someone in your life you hate too much to ever love? Maybe you dislike someone enough to complain about her or him to your friends. Whether you hate or dislike, you are living in a hell. You are in it each time you feel your hatred or dislike.

The journey out of a personal hell requires giving to, caring for, and loving what is most difficult to give to, care for, or love—your hated enemy.

To be compassionate requires that you share your passion with others. The passion of so many now is one of pain, of shock, of grieving, and of loss. Compassion allows you to feel those difficult emotions and the pain that lies beneath them.

It is easier to become enraged and to seek revenge, or swear that you will, than it is to experience the pain of your loss, the depth of your loss, your grief, and your fear.

If you do not experience your emotions and the depth of the pain within you when violence strikes, you will find yourself irresistibly and self-righteously drawn to thoughts of revenge.

The first step in the creation of compassion is to be compassionate with yourself. Allow yourself to feel all that you are feeling. If you are feeling hatred, do not hate yourself for hating.

F eeling hate does not mean acting on it. It means taking the first step in allowing yourself to become conscious of everything that you are feeling so that you can expand your consciousness to the fear and pain that lie beneath the impulses to hate and to seek revenge.

When you think of "terrorists" or remember the Twin Towers collapsing with thousands of people inside, are you in danger of losing your compassion? When you fear that someone will attack you because you are not like them, are you in danger of losing your compassion? Will you become like them—a rigid person who sees "enemies" and has no compassion for them?

It takes courage to fight a war in a dry and cold desert, but how dry and cold is your heart when you hate, when you need revenge, when you want someone to die? That is the desert in which you will fight your greatest battle and, if you are brave enough, win it.

We are all going to die. That is our common destination. We are fellow sailors on the way to the same port. How long the voyage will last is different for all. It is for each of us to decide how we shall make the voyage, and what we shall gain from it.

Sooner or later you will reach the end of your journey through the Earth school. Will you arrive grateful and wise, caring for your fellow travelers and receiving the care that they have for you, or will you arrive complaining about them and about the trip?

We will die, and we will each choose a response to this realization, whether we want to or not. Is there a better response than to turn your attention to the quality of your life?

life of quality is a life of care for other people, a life of integrity, and a life of receiving as well as giving. It is a life lived consciously, courageously, compassionately, and wisely.

Do you love the truth more than you need to be loved, or do you need to be loved more than you love the truth?

Learning how to find what is true for you and share it with sensitivity is the path that each of us is on. No one can get off the path. The path is your life. The only question is how long you will walk on the path before you realize where it is leading you, and appreciate what is on it.

Soul questions come from a deeper place than other questions in our lives. They reach toward meaning and fulfillment.

Soul questions do not concern themselves with the functional aspects of a life, such as projects and careers. They cannot be answered with numbers or theories.

Soul questions are doorways through which soul-to-soul communication enters your life and transforms it.

All soul questions have in common the longing for the vertical path through life—transformation, deeper meaning, fulfillment, and love—rather than the horizontal path—more anger, more success, more recognition, more wealth, more influence, etc.

Answers to your soul questions come from the Universe, and you recognize them by your resonance with what you hear, read, or intuit.

Every soul-to-soul communication benefits all souls. Personalities have different challenges, but all souls have the same intentions—harmony, cooperation, sharing, and reverence for Life.

Just as a new language gives you new freedom of expression and insight, the new multisensory perceptions that are becoming central to the human experience and the new vocabulary that accompanies them allow you to explore in new and surprising ways your own experiences and the depth, power, and meaning of your life.

When you look into a mirror you see only your reflection. When you recognize wisdom, wherever or however that happens for you, it is your wisdom that is being reflected back to you.

Rejecting—for any reason—what you recognize to be significant for you invalidates your own experience, your own power, and the impulses of your own heart.

Do not look for footnotes in matters of the heart and soul. Look inside yourself. Otherwise, you will always be looking for references from others and longing to know how they know what they know.

A new species is being born inside each of us, no matter where we live, what language we speak, or what we do. Eventually, we will all express the new perceptions and values of this new species.

When you hear something that you recognize as true for you, try it out. If it works, incorporate it into your life and use it.

We are learning to draw upon ourselves for answers that we need, because what worked in the past no longer works. Old ways now lead only to painful consequences.

Becoming our own authorities means becoming Teachers to ourselves and to one another. It is now our responsibility to learn how to feel, to listen from the heart, to share from the heart, and to co-create in spiritual partnership—partnership among equals for the purpose of spiritual growth.

Becoming your own authority means finding Teachers inside yourself, and learning to value what you experience. It also means seeing the world around you as a teacher, and learning to value what you hear and see.

vil is an absence. It is not a presence. Evil is the absence of Love—uncontaminated conscious Light.

The difference between judgment of evil and recognition of evil is your emotional reaction. If you are repulsed and frightened, you judge what you encounter. If you can see an angry, deceitful, or violent person for what he or she is—a fellow student in the Earth school who is in extreme pain—you can interact with that person appropriately.

When you have an emotional reaction to what you see, you are judging. That is your signal that you have an issue inside of yourself—with yourself—not necessarily with the other person.

If you react righteously to evil, look inside yourself for the very thing that so agitates you, and you will find it. If it were not there, you would simply discern, act appropriately, and move on.

Your emotional reactions to the evil you encounter and your judgments of it show you what you need to change in yourself. Changing those parts of your personality that judge, react in fear, and cannot love into acceptance, fearlessness, and love is the journey you were born to make.

When you die, you don't go to sleep. You go home to nonphysical reality, and you are very much awake.

Maybe you will make the big changes in this lifetime that are necessary to experience and share love. You can, if you want to. Maybe you will take many lifetimes, but sooner or later, you will make them. When you become completely loving and kind—without fear and without thought of harming others— you graduate from the Earth school. That is when reincarnation ends.

I t is not possible to provide evidence of
life after death to the five senses any
more than it is possible to provide the five
senses with evidence of nonphysical reality. The five senses together form a single
sensory system whose object of detection
is physical reality.

Multisensory perception does not replace five-sensory perception. It adds to it. Multisensory humans perceive physical circumstances, but they also see meaning in them that five-sensory humans do not.

Multisensory humans do not deduce or conclude meaning in their five-sensory circumstances. They perceive it directly.

Multisensory humans feel what is appropriate for themselves regardless of what their five senses tell them and their intellects conclude. Learning to use multisensory perception requires the openness to experiment with your inner sense of knowing when you feel it. That knowing is your access to nonphysical reality.

Nonphysical reality is your home. It is where you came from when you were born and where you will return when you die.

T he word "Universe" refers to Divine Intelligence—to the living, boundless Universe of compassion and wisdom.

There is only one Universe. All the parts of the Universe are One.

No thought is unheard and no prayer goes unanswered, although not always in the way that you expect.

The Universe does not burden you with a destiny. It provides you with potential. How much of that potential you realize depends upon the choices that you make.

A person who speaks rudely to you gives you an opportunity to choose how you will respond. Will you withdraw emotionally? Will you become angry? Will you be able to see his or her fear and pain and respond appropriately?

The optimal choice that you can make in any situation is to grow spiritually. That means intending to create harmony, sharing, cooperation, and reverence for Life.

Thoughts open you or close you. The thought that the Universe is your friend opens you. The thought that your marriage might dissolve closes you. The thought that you are your own source of well-being opens you.

Your thoughts determine whether you will fear and resist your experiences, or whether you will embrace them and be supported by them.

Choosing your thoughts is like choosing a pair of glasses. One pair has dark lenses that make everything appear distorted and threatening. Another pair gives everything that you see a comforting, golden glow. Their lenses do not distort, but help you to see more clearly. When you wear these glasses, all of your experiences appear friendly.

Your five senses cannot provide you with an experience of the Universe as alive, wise, and compassionate. Multisensory perception can.

I ntuition is replacing rational analysis as the primary decision-making tool in the human experience.

Humanity is becoming a heart-centered species instead of a head-centered species.

We are now beginning to see power as the alignment of the personality with the soul instead of the ability to manipulate and control.

The Earth school is not a concept. The Earth school is an ongoing three-dimensional, full-color, high-fidelity, interactive multimedia experience that does not end until your soul goes home— until you die.

Every moment in the Earth school offers you an opportunity to learn important things about yourself that you need to know in order to grow in wisdom and compassion.

When you focus your attention on creating the goals of your soul, your endeavors become spiritual.

The goals of your soul are harmony, cooperation, sharing, and reverence for Life. When those goals become your goals, your personality is aligned with your soul. That is authentic power.

Authentic power is the experience of being grateful to be alive, even during difficult times. Your life is filled with meaning and purpose. Your creativity is unlimited. You enjoy yourself and others. You are fulfilled and fulfilling. You treasure Life in all its forms.

Y ou were born to be a spiritual person.

Growing older does not mean automatically becoming gentler or wiser. Millions of people die angry, frightened, and jealous. If you do not change yourself, you will be one of them. No one can change you except you.

You cannot be a spiritually evolved person and an emotionally unevolved person at the same time.

The first step toward spiritual growth is to become aware of your emotions.

It is difficult to become emotionally aware because many of your emotions are painful—but they offer you the opportunities you need to grow spiritually.

The life of each individual is sacred, although he or she may not be aware of it.

When you take time to know your-self, or to appreciate your life and the lives of others, you open yourself to the experience of the sacred.

L earning to honor the sacred every-where you see it, and learning to see it everywhere, is spiritual development.

The type of certainty that the scientific method provides can help you to survive. It cannot help you to grow spiritually.

Spiritual growth requires the development of inner knowing and inner authority. It requires the heart, not the intellect.

Authentic power is the development of the ability to speak, act, and live with the certainty that your words, actions, and life are appropriate while at the same time allowing others to do the same.

No one's destiny is written. At any moment you can leave the life path that you are now on and embark on one that is more compassionate, wise, fulfilling, and free.

What is behind your eyes is more important than what is in front of them.

You cannot change the reflection in a mirror without changing what the mirror reflects. The mirror is the world that you live in, and it reflects you.

Relationships illuminate parts of your personality that are unhealed—such as the parts that strive to dominate others, please others, judge others, and exploit them—as well as healthy parts of your personality, such as those that are caring, patient, appreciative, and grateful.

If you are in a relationship and "fall in love" with someone else, or think that you have found the one and only person you were destined to be with, or who will complete you, or fulfill you, ask yourself if you are running from the issues that have surfaced in your current relationship.

Does the idea of a new relationship affect you the way that an anesthetic affects an individual in physical pain?

Changing relationships without coming to terms with the parts of your personality that created your present relationship is like changing props on a stage. The play continues. Only the scenery is different.

When you can resist the impulse to criticize, object, explain, clarify, withdraw, or become angry, you will be surprised at how painful some of the physical sensations in your body are, and how proficient you can become at feeling those sensations, observing them, and learning from them. That is how to develop emotional awareness.

Anger and resentment are magnetically attractive, because you cannot be a victim without them.

Forgiveness is something you do for yourself, not for another person.

Forgiveness is letting go of your resentment, disappointment, anger, and hurt. When you do, they no longer intrude on your thoughts and your sleep.

If you forgive, but continue to resent, you have not forgiven. Forgiving is choosing a light and happy heart.

L ove is not something you fall into. It is not a sentimental feeling. It must be cultivated and developed. It requires patience and dedication. It is your ability to care about others.

You cannot act in love and act in fear at the same time. You must choose between them.

There are times when you delight in your partner's strength. There are times when his or her vulnerabilities bring out your most caring tenderness. This is how we were meant to be with each other. It is natural to love.

Judgment is accompanied by a painful emotional reaction. You would like a person or situation to be different. You have expectations that are not satisfied. When that happens, you lose energy.

Discerning is seeing a person or a circumstance as it is. You notice jealousy, for example, or anger, greed, or callousness in another person without being affected by it, just as you notice the color of a flower or the shape of a rock without being affected by it. You do not lose energy.

J udging is seeing yourself as superior or
inferior to another person.

Judgment has an emotional charge to it. It makes one a victim and another a villain.

Judging is like watching a big-screen, big-sound, full-color feature film in black and white on a tiny television set with one small speaker. The feature film is your life. The reduced black-and-white version of it is what you see through your judgments.

Telling a friend that he is judgmental is a judgment that you make about your friend.

If you say to a friend, "When you speak to me like that, my stomach hurts," your friend cannot disagree. At the same time, you have shared some of your experience in a way that he or she might be able to hear.

Becoming upset when you see some-one doing something that you do but don't know that you do is called "projec-tion." You always dislike in others what you don't recognize, or don't want to rec-ognize, in yourself.

Spiritual growth requires becoming aware of everything that you are feeling, and learning about yourself from what you feel.

When you do not take your interactions so personally, you will be
able to see that each offers you a choice—to
see yourself as a victim who reacts to the
circumstances of your life, or as a creator
who chooses your responses to them.

Experiment with allowing yourself to choose your response the next time you feel drawn into the turbulence of others instead of reacting without awareness of your thoughts, feelings, and intention.

Conflicts with parents contain the most potential for spiritual growth. You and your parents are more than conflicting personalities. You are souls that are interacting by choice in the Earth school.

The next time you judge a parent or feel judged by one, ask yourself, "What can I learn about myself from this experience?" If you shift your attention from what is lacking in your parents to what your interactions with them can provide you to develop spiritually, you will begin to develop the very strengths that you need in order to give the gifts that you were born to give.

There is no vocabulary that can communicate sophisticated ideas as clearly to young children as those ideas can be communicated to adults. To teach children, you must model what you want to teach.

When you learn to teach by example as well as with words, you will be much more effective with everyone, and especially with children.

Teenagers, in particular, are sensitive to issues of responsibility because such issues are often used to manipulate them into desired behaviors.

When parents say, "When are you going to grow up?" or, "When I was your age . . ." they create resistance to the idea of responsibility because that idea becomes accurately identified in the experience of the teenager with manipulation.

Allow your insights and inspiration to come in the ways that they will, even if that is not how you think they should come.

Speak from your heart. Don't intellectualize, theorize, or hypothesize, but share what is important to you in a personal and considerate way.

Some foods have higher vibrations than others, which means they have more energy than others.

U ncooked organic vegetables have the most energy, and highly cooked, highly processed foods with added chemicals have the least.

Listen to what your body wants. That will show you your addictions—to caffeine, to sugar, or to nicotine, for example—and also show you what gives you energy and strength.

Many people refuse to eat meat, yet they daily ingest their judgments of others or themselves, critical thoughts, anger, resentment, jealousy, and fear. These are poisons. Why eat pure foods when nothing else you ingest is healthy?

Many people who eat meat have a relationship with Life that is reverent and that respects the natural exchange of energy between the domains of Life on the Earth—mineral, vegetable, animal, and human.

When you are a fountain of love, you do not need to ask for it. You are a source of it.

Your joy in having a vital body is a natural expression of inner health. Your compulsion to have a healthy body is an expression of fear.

I t is natural to run for the pleasure of it, to dance, and to walk in the sun. It is natural to breathe deeply, stretch fully, and move through your life with a limber body and a limber mind.

As you move through the stages of your life, honor your body.

Depression is the surface manifestation of a deep, multilayered dynamic. It is painful beyond what those who have not experienced it can imagine, yet it covers even more painful experiences that need to be unearthed and healed.

If you use the times of relief that anti-depressants provide to look deeply into your life, they will be an aid to you. If you use them to return to the same unexamined life that created your depression, they will be a crutch that you will find increasingly undependable.

Depression, like every painful experience, brings your attention to what needs to be changed in you, by you.

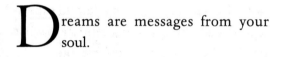

Dreams are messages from your soul.

Dreams are comments on your life. They are valuable perspectives that are meant to inform you of what you need to consider at the moment.

If you do not understand the message your soul is bringing to you in a dream, your next dream the same night will repeat the message, and the next, throughout the night, each conveying the same meaning, which has to do with you and your life. You will receive more messages the next night, and the next, for the duration of your time in the Earth school.

Your life is an opportunity to give the gifts that your soul wants to give.

Your time on the Earth is an opportunity to use your will intelligently, wisely, and compassionately. When you do, you become a conduit for the energy of your soul.

Everything in the Universe moves toward ever-increasing awareness and freedom.

Everything in the Universe, including you, your soul, everyone else, and every soul, participates in a continual unfolding of potential.

E very personality in the Earth school
has lessons to learn and gifts to give.

If you choose cruelty, self-interest, and exploitation, the consequences of your choices—violence and destruction—will appear perfectly in your life, offering you opportunities to grow into greater freedom and awareness. If you choose kindness, care for others, and contribution to Life, the consequences of your choices—contentment and wholeness—will also appear perfectly in your life, offering you opportunities to grow into greater freedom and awareness.

Your soul is at the center of all that you experience. It is your essence. It is the part of you that is immortal.

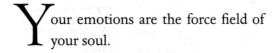

Your emotions are the force field of your soul.

There is perfection in each experience.

Your personality is that part of you that was born on a certain date and will die on a certain date.

Your personality is a tool of your soul.

Your soul is that part of you that existed before you were born and that will continue to exist after you die.

When your personality dies, your soul returns to its home. Its home is nonphysical reality.

A soul leaves the Earth school when it is ready to leave. When a soul decides to go home, nothing can stop it. Until then, nothing can make it return home.

As long as you live on the Earth you will have a personality—a body, a mind, and an intuitional structure, which is your particular way of experiencing intuition.

The purpose of a journey through the Earth school is to discover the frightened parts of your personality and heal them, and to discover the loving parts of your personality and cultivate them.

When you feel resentment, anger, or other painful emotions, it is because you have encountered a part of your personality that is not integrated and whole. Becoming integrated and whole is the spiritual path. Your personality is your vehicle.

As individuals become multisensory, their perceptual capabilities expand beyond the limitations of the five senses, and soul-to-soul communication becomes possible.

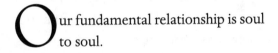

Our fundamental relationship is soul to soul.

There is greatness in every personality that lives the intentions of its soul. It develops humbleness, clarity, forgiveness, and love.

A personality that uses its influence to create harmony where there was discord, sharing where there was hoarding, cooperation where there was competition, and contribution to Life where there was exploitation of Life creates authentic power.

You do not need to become a "great soul" in order to leave the Earth school. You will leave the Earth school when you die.

Multisensory perception, among other things, is the ability to see meaning in everyday circumstances.

As you become multisensory, you also become intuitive.

Intuition is the voice of the nonphysical world.

You access nonphysical guides and Teachers through your intuition. You "hear" them through your insight, inspiration, and clarity.

Nonphysical Teachers cannot make your choices for you. They can only guide you to the full scope and depth of your power. How you choose to use your power is up to you.

Your intellect will rationalize what you want to do. Your intuition will often surprise you.

Intuition broadens your perception and understanding. It enables you to move more fully into your own power and authority.

Paranoia contracts your consciousness. It is compulsive. It expresses the most insecure parts of your personality, separates you from others, and is painful.

Intuition shows you avenues to health.
Paranoia deprives you of health.

Intuition offers you choices. Paranoia imposes choices upon you.

A habit is a repetitive behavior—such as drinking coffee each morning, watching TV in the evening, or wearing certain clothes on certain days—that masks uncomfortable feelings from you. If you intentionally do not do these behaviors, you begin to feel anxious or uncomfortable.

Addictions are behaviors that mask emotions which are so painful that you feel an irresistible urge to do something—such as shop, smoke, gamble, take a drug, watch pornography, drink alcohol, or have sex—rather than experience them.

All unconscious behaviors, including addictions, mask painful emotions. Addicts do not think in terms of avoiding painful emotions. Instead they feel an overpowering, irresistible attraction to sex, alcohol, a cigarette, etc.

Your addictions are your greatest inadequacies. They are the parts of your personality that are out of your control.

Your addiction is not stronger than who you want to become.

The first step in healing an addiction is to acknowledge that you have it.

Once you have seen that a part of yourself is out of control, you must choose to leave it out of control or do something about it. That is the power of acknowledging an addiction.

Your intention to heal your addictions is a necessary and significant step in your spiritual development.

The healing of an addiction is the beginning of a story, not the end of one.

Each individual uncovers different things about himself or herself on the journey of healing, but everyone who takes it emerges transformed from an individual who flees the present moment into one who lives in the present moment gratefully.

All of the behaviors that most need to be changed feel involuntary. They are your obsessions, your compulsions, and, strongest of all, your addictions.

All painful emotions, and the reactions that they create in you, feel involuntary. That is because they originate in parts of your personality that are operating outside the field of your awareness.

Behaviors in yourself that appear to you to be involuntary are the places to start your spiritual journey. They are the flags that tell you that you have inner work to do.

As you become aware of the unconscious parts of your personality and begin to challenge them you will find that, although their power is strong, the behaviors that they desire are not involuntary. They are subject to your will. The more you challenge them, the more they lose power over you. Eventually their power over you disintegrates.

Your responsibility to friends and family members who are addicts is to remain balanced and centered.

The addict, who is always in emotional pain, will attempt to convince you, blame you, reason with you, shout at you, or control you in any way he can into accepting his painful emotional reality. If you accept his blame, reasoning, or control, you assist your friend in the continuation of his addiction and the prolongation of his pain.

An addict's words and behavior are all focused on avoiding exploration of the causes of his addiction and emotional pain. That exploration begins with the idea of self-responsibility—entertaining the possibility that he has created what he is experiencing.

The idea of self-responsibility frequently causes explosive denial on the part of the addict or emotionally distressed individual. That is where your balance and clarity are needed.

Karma is neither good nor bad. Karma is the experience of what you have created.

K arma is the law of cause and effect
through which you shape your life
with every decision.

You may feel that the Universe is treating you badly, but it is not. When you create suffering, you experience suffering. When you create joy, you experience joy.

Asking why the Universe is treating you badly when you experience painful circumstances in your life is like asking a mirror why you look the way that you do. Your reflection will not change until you change. Karma is your reflection.

Affirmations and visualizations are effective only when they are used to focus an intention.

When you set the intention to respond compassionately to everything that you experience, you allow your Karma to open your heart rather than close it.

Karma is a gift from the Universe. As your awareness grows, it will become a gift that you cherish.

You cannot interfere with someone else's Karma. You can only make your own Karma.

Everything that you do is a choice and every choice that you make creates experiences that you will encounter. That is Karma.

Doing what you can to protect the molested from the molester is appropriate. Judging the molester is not. Protecting the oppressed is appropriate. Judging the oppressor is not.

Do you have the courage to protect without judging? Can you be compassionate even to those who have no compassion? If so, there is no finer Karma that you can create.

The first step in challenging a painful emotion is to become aware of it. If you do not challenge your anger, fear, or jealousy, you will die with it.

U nless you heal the parts of your personality that are causing you pain,
they will not change. No one can change
them but you.

Your anger, jealousy, and other painful experiences are your avenues to spiritual growth.

When you set the intention to heal your anger—or jealousy, anxiety, vengefulness, or any other fear—the aspect of yourself that you challenge comes to the foreground of your consciousness. You begin to experience it more frequently so that you can challenge it more frequently. If you look at every recurrence of a frightened part of your personality as a setback, you do not recognize the power of your intention.

Your anger or jealousy or fear does not disappear the first time you challenge it, or the second or the third. Gaining power over these parts of your personality requires you to challenge them again and again and yet again.

When you challenge your anger—
or jealousy, vengefulness, etc.—it
appears to increase, but it does not. Your
awareness of it, and the number of opportunities that you have to challenge it, have
increased.

It is not possible to repress an emotion
and challenge it simultaneously.

To challenge a frightened part of your personality effectively, you must be able to recognize every aspect of it—where you feel it in your body, what kind of thoughts it creates, and what impulses it generates. Only then will you be able to begin the process of coming to terms with it.

By paying close attention to the frightened parts of your personality—the parts that are angry, impatient, jealous, etc.—and learning every detail about them, you will know exactly what you want to change about yourself.

The only change you will experience in your life is the change you choose to make.

Only the intention to change yourself can change you, and you are the only one who can hold that intention.

When you choose to create harmony, cooperation, sharing, and reverence for Life, you activate all the parts of your personality that prevent you from creating those things so that you can recognize them and heal them, one by one, choice by choice, decision by decision, as they arise.

The unexpected is the great teacher
of flexibility, adaptability, and trust.

The frequency and intensity of emotional reactions to the unexpected is an indicator of the degree of trust in the Universe that is present or absent.

When you resist change, you experience emotional pain and physical pain. When you welcome change, you relax and open to new possibilities. Resistance is an experience of fear and doubt, and openness is an experience of love and trust.

Nonphysical Teachers are impersonal sources of wisdom and compassion that are real but not physical.

It is not the job of your nonphysical Teachers to make you compassionate and wise. That is your job.

You can use your time on this pre-cious Earth complaining about what others are doing on it, or consciously deter-mining what you are doing on it.

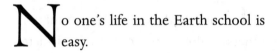

No one's life in the Earth school is easy.

When you judge an experience as unfair, or tragic, or random, you automatically experience anger, emotional withdrawal, depression, fear, or another of the many painful emotions that accompany the perception of yourself as a victim.

When you see each of your challenges as an opportunity to discover and change the parts of your personality that feel like a victim rather than the creator of your own experiences, you automatically respond to the challenges in your life with gratitude, and even joy.

You go nowhere in your life by continuing to respond to difficulties in the same ways that you have responded to them in the past. Your experiences change when your responses to your challenges change.

The circumstances of your life are neither good nor bad. They are appropriate to the needs of your soul. They may or may not be what your personality desires.

Positioning yourself as a victim who deserves better than you are receiving prevents you from using your life as it was designed to be used—to grow spiritually.

Regret serves no useful function in spiritual growth. It makes the tree grow crooked. It keeps you imprisoned in the role of a victim—in this case, of your own choices—instead of learning from your painful experiences so that you do not repeat them.

Some experiences are painful to remember because, as you look back on them, you see how you could have spoken or acted otherwise, or how you wish things would have turned out differently. The purpose of these memories is to instruct you, not torment you.

Relive your painful experiences not to dive once more into trauma and agony, but to discover what intentions you held at the time, and to examine the words that you spoke, and your actions. Compare what you created then with what you want to create now, and use your experiences to help you create differently.

Once you have learned from your painful memories and you feel confident in your intentions to apply what you have learned from them to your life, release them.

Imagine each one of your painful memories and thoughts as a helium balloon, and that you are holding the strings. Then imagine cutting the strings with a pair of scissors and watching the balloons rising up and up, getting smaller and smaller, until they disappear.

A person's competitive nature often expresses itself by making comparisons of oneself, one's house, or one's children as better or worse than others. The underlying issue is not competitiveness, but fear—the insecurity that expresses itself in the need to compete.

The pain of ending a relationship that you want to keep comes from experiencing the difference between how you would like the world to be and how the world is.

Learning to let go of your pain, accept, and move on without a partner who no longer wants to continue a relationship with you requires that you look inside yourself to see what part you played in creating the experience. For example, ask yourself what expectations you had, and whether those expectations were perhaps a burden for your partner.

You can learn more about yourself from the painful experience of ending a relationship than you can about your partner. And you can change yourself with what you learn, but you cannot change your partner. That is for your partner to do.

Forgiveness is an energy dynamic. When you forgive, you lighten your load. Forgiveness is putting down all of your baggage and leaving it behind. You travel lightly.

Not forgiving is like wearing dark sunglasses that gruesomely distort all that you see, and wanting others to see through the same glasses.

Forgiveness has nothing to do with worthiness—yours or others'. The issue is whether you wish to continue to carry your baggage.

J ust as you cannot learn how to ride a
bicycle before you begin to ride, you
cannot learn to trust without experiment-
ing with trusting.

Trusting requires you to entertain the idea that nothing happens without a reason, and that reason has to do with your spiritual growth.

To become the person you want to be, you must decide what it is about yourself that you want to change, and how to do that.

When you decide to change, that change has already begun.

Try to create harmony instead of discord, cooperation instead of competition, sharing instead of hoarding, and contributing to others instead of taking from them.

E xperiment with your life. That is what you have it for.

Every human being has a sacred contract that he or she voluntarily entered into with the Universe. Your responsibility while you are in the Earth school is to create authentic power. That enables you to give the gifts that you were born to give, and that is how you fulfill your sacred contract.

When you feel that your life has no purpose and you do not know why you are alive, you are not doing what your soul wants you to do.

When you know that you are alive for a reason and that what you are doing serves that reason, you are filled with enthusiasm, joy, and gratitude. Everything becomes meaningful and worthy of your attention. That is the experience of authentic power.

I f what you are doing is not satisfying to you, or exciting, or fulfilling, try something else. The more authentic power you develop, the more freedom you will have to experiment with your life, and the more desire you will have to experiment with it.

The single best thing you can do for yourself is to realize that you are worthy of your life and to live it accordingly.

The experience of the equality of all forms of Life is reverence.

When reverence becomes central to the human experience, the exploitation of all forms of Life by the human species, including the exploitation of humans by humans, will cease.

The creation of authentic power requires that you distinguish between your artificial needs and your authentic needs.

You have an authentic need to express
the love that is within you, your care
and affection for Life, your concern for the
Earth, and your desire to be in companion-
ship with others. The size of your car or
home, the color of your clothes, and the
cut of your hair are not authentic needs.

Satisfying your authentic needs serves the intentions of your soul and feeds your soul. You are grateful for what you have and you have what you need. A large house can be the fulfillment of an artificial need—a need created by fear—or a tool that you have acquired in your pursuit of authentic power.

You cannot run away from the lessons that you need to learn. When you learn them, there is no longer anything to run away from.

Awareness is the key that allows temptation to lose power, to make that which is unconscious conscious.

Temptation is a dress rehearsal for a negative Karmic event. It is a gift from the Universe that enables you to see negativity in yourself that would create painful consequences if it were allowed to remain unconscious.

Recognizing your intention when you act is important because your intentions, not your actions, create the consequences that you will experience.

If you donate money to charities because you want to be known as a generous person, or to think of yourself as generous, your intention is to gain, not to give.

I f your intention is to give, you will not be concerned with how your actions are perceived.

Emotional withdrawal is a form of pursuing external power. It is an attempt to manipulate and control.

When you pursue authentic power, you do not hold others responsible for your experiences.

Doubt is the absence of trust.

The question of whether you will learn wisdom through fear and doubt or through love and trust is the one that confronts every individual every moment of every day.

Authentic power is the experience of creating with an empowered heart without attachment to the outcome.

You cannot feel as though your life is purposeful, meaningful, and creative when you are sad, frightened, angry, jealous, or vengeful.

By looking for the wisdom and the compassion that is waiting for you in your most difficult experiences, you will change your life.

The difficult situations in your life provide you with opportunities to be patient with others instead of becoming angry or judgmental, and to speak from your heart instead of your head, which means to speak from the most grounded, healthy, and appropriate place you can find in yourself.

The exploration of authentic power does not require abandoning your faith. Jews, Hindus, Muslims, Buddhists, Christians, and nonreligious people all seek meaning, purpose, and fulfillment. They long to live joyfully and to contribute all that they can to Life. These are the experiences of authentic power.

B e open to what your experiences tell
you about yourself, rather than what
they might tell you about other people.

Notice what you do not like about other people, because your reactions to them can show you parts of your personality that you are not aware of, or that you have been avoiding.

You cannot grow spiritually without relationships of substance and depth.

Humbleness, clarity, forgiveness, and love are the characteristics of an authentically empowered personality.

A species-wide spiritual awakening is taking place. The door to new dimensions of consciousness is opening for millions, and soon will open for all. What you do with your new consciousness is for you to decide.

# AN INVITATION TO THE
# SEAT OF THE SOUL INSTITUTE

I would like to extend to you a warm welcome to join me on an exciting journey to the soul. In this amazing time of spiritual awakening, the door to new dimensions of consciousness is now opening before millions of us, and soon will open for all. What you do with your new consciousness is for you to decide, and no one can decide it for you. When you choose to align your personality with your soul—to create harmony, cooperation, sharing, and reverence for Life—you create authentic power.

Authentic power is the experience of meaning, vitality, creativity, and joy. Humbleness, clarity, forgiveness, and love are the characteristics of an authentically empowered individual. Creating authentic power requires emotional awareness, because your emotions are the force field of your soul; conscious choice of your intentions, because they create your experiences; consulting your intuition, because it can show you options you might not have considered and their respective consequences; and trust in the Universe. It also requires commitment, courage, compassion, and conscious communications and actions.

My spiritual partner, Linda Francis, and I have created the Seat of the Soul Institute. Its vision is a world in which spiritual growth is the highest priority, and all of its programs and activities are designed to support you in creating authentic power and spiritual partnerships.

Please visit us at

www.seatofthesoul.com

and learn how our activities and programs can support you in creating authentic power. Also, please feel free to email me at

gary@seatofthesoul.com.

We are all now on the journey to the soul. I hope to see you sometime soon.

Love,
Gary Zukav